AF449068

JACOB AND THE CLOUD

KELSEY IRVING

EMELINE LEYENS

POP! The piñata exploded and candy spilled down. The party guests squealed with excitement as they collected their favorite candies. Jacob charged in as well, but he didn't shout or even smile. Something was holding him back from having fun.

It was a big dark cloud.

Jacob stepped up to the slide, but the cloud got in his way. He sat at the base of the ladder and sighed.

Jacob tried to draw with chalk on the sidewalk, but the cloud blocked the sun and made it hard to see what he was doing. He clenched his jaw and tried to shoo the cloud away.

When Jacob tried to play soccer with his friends, the cloud rested heavily on his shoulders, making it difficult to run. He hung his head and kicked at the grass.

One morning Jacob woke up and peeked out from under his covers and whispered, "Is the cloud here?"

"Oh no! Go away, cloud. I don't want you here."

TOYS

At school, Jacob looked over his shoulder. The cloud was still there. "Ugh! I wish you would leave me alone." Jacob's hands felt sweaty and he was getting a stomach ache.

Jacob slumped his shoulders and said to the cloud, "No matter how hard I try to get rid of you, you never go away."

The next day, Jacob expected the cloud to come along to soccer practice as it always did. Instead of thinking about ways to get rid of the cloud, he tried to focus on kicking the ball and playing with his friends. At first it was really hard, but the more Jacob focused on the game, the less he was bothered by the cloud.

Jacob noticed the cloud less and less. "I've done it!" He exclaimed. "I beat the cloud!"

But the next day, the cloud was back, floating patiently nearby. Although he was upset at first, Jacob said, "Fine, you can come along. I can still play with my friends even if you're with me."

So the cloud went along with Jacob, as it always did, but there was one big difference: Jacob stopped trying to get rid of it. Instead, he allowed it to be there.

Whether the cloud was big or small, it did not keep Jacob from doing the things that were important to him.

One day, Jacob got onto the bus to go to school. He sat waiting for a friend, but as he looked around, he noticed that one of his classmates seemed to have a weight on her shoulders. She sighed, clenched her jaw, kicked at the ground, and finally tried to shoo something away. Jacob knew what that meant.

He gulped. He had never spoken to the girl before, but the cloud had made him realize that he could do hard things.

He leaned across the aisle.
"Hi, I'm Jacob. Are you ok?"
"I don't know. It's this big stinky cloud above me. It ruins my day."

"Oh! I have a cloud too, see? I used to not like my cloud because I thought it kept me from doing stuff, but I learned that I can still do all the things I like, even when the cloud is there. We pretty much go everywhere together."

"Lots of people have clouds. Even grownups have clouds sometimes."

"Sometimes the cloud can go away for a while. And sometimes it comes back."

"But instead of trying to shoo it away or ignore it, I let it be there while I carry on with my day."

The girl looked at her cloud thoughtfully.
"Hmm, maybe I can try that."

When the bus stopped and the girl walked away, Jacob waved. He turned to the cloud. "Maybe having you around is not so bad after all."

RESOURCES

In 2022, nearly 7 million children and 50 million adults in America are experiencing a mental illness. With so many Americans being affected, there is more research being done and more resources than ever! To learn more about how you can help yourself or your child, be sure to check out these resources:

National Alliance on Mental Illness - NAMI.org
The Happiness Trap - thehappinesstrap.com
The International OCD Foundation - iocdf.org
Anxiety and Depression Association of America - adaa.org
Kids Health - kidshealth.org

If you or someone you know is having thoughts of suicide or self harm, help is available. Call or text 988 to connect with the 988 Suicide & Crisis Lifeline. The Lifeline provides 24-hour, confidential support to anyone in suicidal crisis or emotional distress. Support is also available via live chat. Para ayuda en español, llame al 988.

ABOUT

THE AUTHOR

Kelsey Irving is a Licensed Mental Health Counselor and owner of Steadfast Psychology Group, a private practice where she specializes in treating clients with OCD and anxiety disorders in Portsmouth, NH. During her years of clinical experience, Kelsey saw significant progress in clients who understood and embraced principles of Acceptance and Commitment Therapy (ACT). As a new mother, Kelsey felt passionate about getting principles of ACT into the hands of young children, and that's how the idea of Jacob and the Cloud was born. Outside of work, Kelsey is an avid skier, aspiring green thumb, and average cook. Learn more at kelseyirvinglpc.com

THE ILLUSTRATOR

Emeline Leyens is an artist in Philadelphia, PA. She is currently working as a freelance designer and artist taking on a range of projects, focusing primarily on graphic/visual design, illustration, and acrylic painting. Emeline's simplified and gestural illustrations were a perfect match for helping to tell the story of Jacob and his cloud. When she's not creating, Emeline is hiking with her dogs, trying new foods with friends, and hanging out with family. Check out some of her recent work at emelineleyens.com, and her art shop at emeline.studio.